The Sprock__ Spaniel

~

If you asked a Springer Spaniel to clamber into a thorny ditch on a wet winter's day, they would say 'But of course'....

If you asked a Cocker Spaniel to charge in, he would turn round and say 'Really? I can tell you right now that there is nothing in there of interest... so no thank you'.

If you asked a Sprocker, they would answer 'I can categorically inform you there is nothing in there for either of us, however I will do it just to make you happy'....

~

By

Anne-Marie Millard

&

Richard Botwright

ISBN-13: 978-1500501112

CONTENTS

DEDICATED TO SPANIELS

This is not the most highbrow book you are going to read on Spaniels, but it is written with love, humour, adoration, general huge good will to all the lovely people we have met and sold Sprockers to over the years; and to the fact that Ernie can throw himself in a pond and then cover me with mud and he is forgiven in a split second. That Flo's face smiles at me hopefully every morning, a ball, a dummy, a lead in mouth and is never disappointed if I say 'no'; that Sprocker puppies move like the wind in a corn field, and shriek like a banshee in a dodgy horror movie. Like all the spaniels I know, they are the loveliest combination of naughtiest and charm, good humour and patience, and, quite truly, man's best friend.

1 THE SPROCKER – AN EXPLANATION

Springer + Cocker = Sprocker

The aforementioned quote would bring a knowing smile to any spaniel owner past, or present. Having had spaniels over the decades between us, we have had ample time to study their quirks, their powers, their abilities to love, infuriate and to make you laugh from all three kinds of the Spaniels involved in this book.

Having started with Springer's quite by mistake – I went to buy a kitten in a North London pet shop and came back with a liver and white dog (as you do) – the years following that incident were full of dog hair and noise as the house slowly filled up with Springer's, Cockers and subsequently Sprocker's.

These days they all have their own respective homes, whether it be in the house, on my Mothers bed or in the kennels. It is now my absolute pleasure that breeding Spaniels is not just my life, but my partners too.

From that one impulse purchase

I never looked back and seeing I spend a lot of time extolling the virtues of Sprocker's to more and more people I felt it was time to showcase them (quite rightfully) in their own book.

I do hope you feel the love, passion and sometimes confusion that we feel about the unsung hero that is a Sprocker. Don't get us wrong – they are not perfect – but they are certainly not far from it!

Tai'

2 A HISTORY

English physician Dr. John Caius described the spaniel in his book the 'Treatise of Englishe Dogs' published in 1576. This was the first mention of the differing British breeds by function. By 1801, Sydenham Edwards explained in the Cynographia Britannica that the land spaniel should be split into two kinds: the Springing or Hawking Spaniel, and the Cocking or Cocker Spaniel.

At this point in time, both cocker and springer spaniels were born in the same litters. The purpose in life of this breed was to serve as a hunting dog. The smaller cockers were used to hunt woodcock, whilst their larger littermates, the Springers spaniels would 'spring' or flush the gamebird into the air where a trained falcon or hawk would bring it to the handler.

Many Spaniel breeds were developed during the 19th century, and often named after the countries where they were developed, or after their owners (who were often nobility). Two types of land Spaniels were predominant and were said to have been of 'true Springer type'. These were the Norfolk and Shropshire Spaniels, and by the 1850's, they were shown under the breed name of the Norfolk Spaniel.

By January 1899, the Spaniel Club of England and the Sporting Spaniel Society held their trials together for the first time. Two years later, in 1902, a combination of the physical standard from the Spaniel Club of England and the abililty standard from the Sporting Spaniel Society led to the English Springer being officially first recognized by the English Kennel Club. The American Kennel club followed suit in 1910.

It is very hard to track down the roots of the Sprocker as a cross between a Springer and a Cocker. As you read it hasn't, in the grand scheme of things, been that long since both Springers and Cockers were born in the same litter.

The general feeling is that Gamekeepers in Scotland began the cross breed to create a dual purpose working field Spaniel for their big estates, combining the best traits of both Spaniel types for flushing across varied ground cover.

Now, finally, the Sprocker is coming into the limelight not just as an excellent multi-tasking working gundog but as a superb family pet. There is a lot of misguided thought that a Sprocker is just a current trend for a designer dog, but this is simply not the case. Firstly the Sprocker is a result of breeding two different types of the same dog (i.e. the Spaniel) and not a cross of two different breeds (i.e. labradoodle which is a Labrador and a poodle) and secondly the Sprocker has long been a secret asset to the shooting world and has taken a while for the breed to be nationally sort after.

Sprockers are turning out to be one of the most popular Spaniels at the moment, with many very active Facebook sites, and websites dedicated purely to them. All of which is a huge bonus for us Sprocker lovers.

Ernie' in contemplative mood

3 A CHARACTER DEFINED

It is terrible to stereotype anybody or anything, and I would guess to try and explain the character of a breed of dog is doing just that. However there are several principles over the years of observing from afar (often muttering under my breath) that I think that you can almost set in stone.

To begin to define a Sprocker, you need to understand the Spaniel. In this case, Springers and Cockers. However, as with any child, the offspring will contain various elements of both parents, some good and possibly some slightly negative. And these traits often don't become apparent until further on in puppyhood.

We have found though, after our own experiences, that the look of a pup can point you in the right direction. Our mainstay Cocker stud is Ted: with a strong bold head, heavyset, muscular with the most naughtiest twinkle in his eye, any pup that has the leanings of their Father, is likely to be as good natured as they come, strong willed with an interest of repositioning shoes around the grounds.

I like to think of Springer's being the 'older sisters' of the group. Poor Springer Spaniels get an awful press: that of being hyperactive and mad with the need to be walked hours daily by an exhausted owner. Rubbish!! You do get the more old fashioned working Springer, whose job in life is to 'work', whether that being on a shooting field or in a park with young kids keeping up their attention, a truly fulfilling life for that particular dog.

But they are not all like that at all. Being with you, being involved in what you do whether it be reading a book or doing the ironing PLUS an interesting walk and playtime is all you need to keep a Springer happy.

The Springer male is the most stoic of the lot. Though he can be the most naughty creature ever when young (just picture 'Just William'), when they mature they settle down and can be endlessly patient, a great protector of those they love, highly sensitive to the mood swings of humans, they often choose to take themselves off to a quiet place if their home is suddenly filled with chaos.

Our male Springer's are usually found tucked beneath our feet, not bothering you or asking for affection (but they do love a full on cuddle), just wanting to know exactly where you are

'Billy' – aka Stonecrop Boy, a fine Springer Dog

and what you are doing. They are the most loyal animal, and can often pine or howl miserably for the first few moments of being alone.

Springer bitches are the Queen's of the castle, refined, elegant, thoughtful and clever, they are not great barkers or howlers, saving their voices for only important announcements. They are magnificent Mothers, very interested in rearranging

'S ally' - aka Glancarw Minnie, one of our liver and white Springer bitches

their off-spring in bundles and piles to suit them. Their tail is constantly wagging, so much so their rear end undulates like a 1950's starlet. Their eyes shine with reflective cheerfulness. I often find I have a trail of Springer girls in a crocodile fashion behind me, if I change direction suddenly I find myself in a sea of girls all greeting me as though I had been away all day.

The Cocker male is the powerhouse of Spaniels. With a hereditary drive to retrieve and to please, we find piles of shoes and suchlike left around the place, whilst they have gone off to look for you, the 'look what I have

Ted' – aka Gunsmoke Goldfinch, our Working Cocker stud

done – am I not just the most clever dog ever?' expression on their face.

Despite being quite low to the ground and stocky compared to their Springer counter parts, they are the most athletic creatures. Steeple chasing is defiantly their forte. They can bounce like Tigger on a good day with eyes shining, glowing with happiness. A cocker male does certainly need exercise, a walk on a lead is not going to be fulfilling for them, they run free in their hunting pattern, running ahead and circling back to you. They need variety to keep both mind and body stimulated.

Finally we bring on the divas. The Cocker girls are true show queens. Never one to miss a conversation with you, their heads leaned to one side, dark eyes staring deep into your soul. They are the most small and

Jade' – aka Lindrob Jade, our beautiful Working Cocker

delicate of all the spaniels we have. Slim, snake hipped, moving like an otter but with the ability to jump into your arms without a moment's notice.

Cocker girls want to be as close to you as possible, wrapping their heads around your neck like a scarf, breathing into the nape of your neck, pressing their small muscular bodies up against you as if trying to merge and become one with you.

And they chat. Boy do they chat! These are defiantly the little sisters of the group, never to miss a trick at being

center of attention. First
they capture your gaze,
hypnotically pulling you
into their world, and then
they start. It's not so
much as a bark but a 'yip',
cross, indignant, excited,
and desperately trying to

'Jade' – aka Lindrob Jade, running free

impart information to you like Morse code. They are not
the dog to have if you live next door to a library....

4 SHOW OR WORKING SPANIELS

We need to go over the difference between 'show' spaniels and 'working' spaniels. Show type dogs are instantly recognizable to most having a typical domed head, longer ears and a rather glamorous high maintenance coat with beautiful feathering. As the name suggests this type of Spaniel can be seen at shows where dogs are judged against the Kennel club breed standard. But just by being a 'show-type' spaniel does not mean that you have to commit to showing your dog only that the dog in question resembles the general type to one degree or another.

Working spaniels have become increasingly popular in the recent years and are no longer confined to just the shooting or field trial set. A working Springer or Cocker will have far less extravagant coat, often with shorter ears. The working line is often smaller with lighter bones and often a bit more 'busy' in nature.

It is working spaniels that we have in our breeding kennels and as pets however 'Bubbles' the Springer has one show dog in her line, which makes her coat far heavier than the other working girls. She is also the

'Bubbles' – aka Gayenor Gun Shaft

most docile of the dogs we have, certainly not the most boring, in fact a complete enigma. However she does require a lot more grooming and general maintenance than her counterparts, most of which she utterly detests. She expects the star treatment, crowds parting in her wake, and toast and brie for breakfast but being groomed is utterly unacceptable .

5 SPROCKER PUPPIES

There is huge explosion of Sprocker puppies out there for you to choose from. But let's have a look at the pros and cons. Often, in the past, Sprockers have been an 'accident' from

an amorous Cocker (or Springer) taking a shine to the next door neighbours female.

Secondly there is the 'working factor', as we have said Gamekeepers and the shooting fraternity have long known the secret of the powers of the Sprocker. These pups will have been bred by choice, from their working gundog lines.

Next are the people that own both a Springer and a Cocker and decide to breed from them, sometimes for their own benefit, to carry on a lineage of their own dogs, and sometimes to sell.

Finally there are established working spaniel breeders (like ourselves) who have a kennel full of Kennel Club registered Spaniels with great pedigrees, which actively choose to use their dogs to produce the best Sprockers they can.

Apart from option number one: none of the above are

actually best avoided. As long as there is honesty and integrity, and you feel that you can ask all the questions necessary then go ahead and see the pups.

The benefit you will get from an established breeder will be advice on what to expect from your puppy from the moment you put a deposit down. You should also get great after service too, and best of all is the ability to get recommendations and reassurance from past puppy buyers.

These are the things you need to think about:

Dog or bitch?

This is a personal opinion, but if I was going to have a one dog family then I would always go for a male. I find them quieter in the long run, and more accepting that life is not always about them, and

'Oscar' owned by the Popplewell family

they seem happier to heave a long suffering sigh and curl up in their bed while you get on with the trivia of everyday life.

BUT not everyone agrees. So think about size: the male Sprocker is always bigger and chunkier than the female. What suits your house, car and general lifestyle? Which do you prefer aesthetically? There is no point pretending that looks are not the key, they are, so slimmer bitch or chunky dog?

Having a bitch will mean you need to have a think about her coming into season twice a year. This usually starts from between six to twelve months. The season lasts roughly three weeks, and  during this time there will be a discharge of blood. This usually starts off quite light, darkens up and then returns towards a light discharge. Most bitches will clean themselves up, some can have almost unnoticeable seasons, but don't be fooled by that, they can still get pregnant. So you need to remember your girl is emitting a highly attractive smell to all the dogs in the neighbourhood, so you might get a lot of unwanted admirer's pawing at the fences!

You can get your bitch spayed which will eliminate all of the above drama. Most vets would recommend this and it is done at an early age, usually just after they have had their first season.

Docked or not docked?

This can be a highly contentious subject and I for one, can understand both sides of the argument. Tail docking is highly regulated in England and currently illegal in Scotland. However the University of Glasgow have written a report on a study they have undertaken which basically says that working dogs and / or dogs that have a lifestyle of running through undergrowth of thorns and bushes should have their tails docked to reduce the risk of injury. If you have ever seen a spaniel with a broken tail then you would understand the argument for the tail to be docked.

The law now stands that the tail must be docked within 72 hours of the puppy's birth; the owner/breeder of the puppy must hold a shotgun or firearms license. All of our working dogs and puppies are docked at our kennels. If a litter is destined as family pets then we do not dock the puppies.

Colours and combinations of Sprockers:

Given the wide variety of Springer's and Cockers, you get the choice of an ever bigger pool of colours, weights, and heights. So whatever colour you can get Cockers in (gold, black,

chocolate, lemon roan, fox red, blue rown, tri-colour) bred with a black and white or liver and white springer you can have a lot of choice out there. The most common and also the most popular colours are chocolate or black with a possibility of some white markings usually the chest and/or the toes.

6 FINDING YOUR PUPPY

The internet is usually the way forward here. However you can also ask at your local vets if they can recommend someone locally and local papers and 'free ads' will give you a lot of choice too. There are lots of websites that you can find adverts on: it is not just the general public that advertises on these, you can find local breeders too. We sell most of our pups through the website though, and have waiting lists for all our litters in place. So a 'google' search for Sprocker breeders is worth it.

Be prepared to travel. A good puppy from good parentage is worth a few hours driving. Avoid bringing your children for your first visit. You need to be sure it's the right breeder and puppy for you, and your kids will only get very excited and make you forget all the questions you wanted to ask.

Be prepared to wait. A good puppy is not going to fall into your perfect time schedule. If you have holidays and family commitments booked then you need to put your puppy buying on hold until you have enough quality time to give the pup a head start in their new life.

We often get requests for puppies who will be ready in time for the school summer holidays. If this is the best time for you, then you need to be working well ahead of yourselves. You can't expect to get the right puppy at the right age, three weeks before you want it. Be looking six months ahead of yourself, get on a good waiting list with the assurance there should be a pup in that litter for you.

A decent phone call is essential – you need have a few questions to hand (easy ones) that can lay the foundation of when you meet the owner / breeder and the puppies.

Here are a few suggestions:

- Will I be able to see the mother (dam) of the litter?
- Can I see the Father (sire)? If not, who is he and where is he?
- Are either the parents Kennel club registered?
- How old are the puppies now?
- When are they ready to leave?
- What do I get for my money?

The last question might seem a bit rude, but you need to know that the puppy will be vet checked and inoculated at eight weeks by the owner. Ideally you want to know the pup was vet checked at birth first and foremost. I would personally insist that your puppy will be checked and vaccinated by a vet before he/she leaves the owner / breeder. This is responsible dog breeding. Many small things can be wrong, none of which you should be dealing with. 'Flow' murmurs in the heart are often detected at the eight week vaccination vet check. These are 99% likely to have disappeared by the last ten – twelve week check.

However you are owed the option of taking that risk or not by the people you are buying from. If there is a flow murmur, you should be informed. We (in the case of a flow murmur) always insist on keeping the puppy until the next vet check and second lot of vaccines.

If the puppy has been docked, the breeder legally has to have the puppy microchiped for you. You have to also be given (again by law) the original legally docked certificate.

If the phone conversation goes well, and you come off the phone excited and eager, then you are off to a good start. If you come away feeling a bit 'wrong' then maybe that's not the puppy for you. Trust your gut instinct.

You can always do a bit of research before you leave, write a list of questions, however silly they sound, they are important to you and therefore must be asked. If the parents are Kennel club registered then you can ask for their pedigree names and/or registration number and have a look for them on the Kennel club website.

Meeting the puppies:

Appearances do matter. Have a look round where the pups are kept, it doesn't matter if it's not all brand new, but does it look clean and looked after? Puppies and kennels do have a certain smell, we get used to it here at ours, but it should not be over powering. The water bowls should be full and clean. Bedding should be so clean that you would happily sit on it.

Puppies can be a little shy to begin with. They don't all come bounding over to see you. Some will sit in a corner observing you, and when they decide you look ok and friendly enough they will wander over to say hello. Don't be put off pups like this, they are just cautiously considering their opinion about you! Some people will say avoid the shyer ones, I don't agree.

I like the idea that some pups (and subsequently dogs) have the ability to think before they act. We don't all want a dog that charges bouncing over to you – especially if you have small kids or you are inexperienced with dogs.

Make sure you meet the mum. Some bitches are quite happy letting you be around their offspring. Some are VERY unhappy about it. If the latter is the case then, you should see the mum with the  pups, watch how they interact together and then most breeders will take the mum away so you can have a closer look.

It is at this point you can ask all of your questions. If you are a novice it is always good to know how much back up you will get from the breeder (whether they be a professional one or just a private family/person) once you have taken the puppy home.

Don't be pushed into anything. If it doesn't feel right, then walk away.

What to look for in your Sprocker:

We have noticed that our Sprocker's, in comparison to the Springer's and Cockers grow at a slower rate and, when people visit, they are often surprised how small they are. Don't be fooled by this, normally around the ten week mark they have a sudden growth spurt and catch up.

You would have in your mind's eye exactly what you want. Have a look at the Mothers features, the length of her nose, and the broadness of her head, her general stance. Is this what you like? Even if she is not

'Izzy B' – aka Kilhopemoss Marionette

the colour way you are after (i.e. she is a liver and white Springer and you are looking at a black bitch pup) her physical characteristics will be inherited. Our Springer 'Sally' for example has a very marked way of sitting, and all her pups seem to inherit this particular trait, even the males.

See if you can have a look at the Sire too. Even if it's not in person then there should photographs available for you to see. Decide which one you prefer and then you can work your way through the pups. We often find that a Sprocker litter are often very difficult to tell apart if they are one colour (i.e. chocolate), their defining features will be the small amounts of white marks on them, more often or not on their bellys, but also they can have white chests, chins, toes and

'Ted' – aka Gunsmoke Gold Finch

occasionally stars on the crown of their heads.

Have a look through those features as well as the shape of the head, and general stance of the pups. Paws can always be a good indicator of the male pups to what size they will grow in comparison to their siblings. Do ask the breeder their opinion too, they have

'Milla' – daughter of Ted and Izzy B – owned by the Thorogood Family

been with this litter from conception until your point of choosing, and they should know the Mother (and often the sire) incredibly well and should be able to see which parent the puppy looks most like.

If the Mother has had a litter before, it can be worth asking to see some photos of her older pups. We keep a lot on file, and there are always updates on our Facebook site, and we find that this is very helpful in narrowing down your choice of pup.

When the litter is smaller, and you have only one or two choices, please don't have the mindset that there is something wrong with the ones left. There isn't anything, it's just 'one of those things'. Our black and white Springer 'Bubbles' was the last of her litter, and so was 'Teddy; our gold cocker, they are the most perfect dogs we could have asked for!

All puppies will be treated and looked after equally by a good breeder, and sometimes having less of a choice makes life a LOT easier when it comes to picking out your perfect pup.

It is perfectly normal to be asked questions by the breeder. They do need to know what experience you have with dogs, where you live, and how much time you have to look after their puppy once it leaves their home. In fact, I would be more than worried if the breeder didn't seem interested in you!

Finally do expect to pay a deposit for your puppy. This is to show your commitment to the pup, and to the breeder. Make sure you get a receipt with an agreed final total to be paid written on it and signed. At this point you just need to double check what you are getting for your money. So be quite clear in asking.

7 PREPARING FOR YOUR SPROCKER PUP

Sprocker's are intensely inquisitive creatures. They particularly like knowing where, what and why of anything and everything. Once they have learnt where everything is, they also

'Coco' owned by the Hollis family

like going back to check nothing has been changed without their approval.

Your first job is to locate the best vet. If you have not had a vet before or experience of one, it's best to seek out advice from other local people. Dog owners love chatting about their animals so if you don't have dog owner friends and neighbours, the local dog walking venue is the best place to accost (and make friends) with other dog owners. You can then either ring the vets up or pop in and get yourself registered with them.

If you are planning on puppy training classes, the same applies as above. These classes get VERY full so think and work ahead on this. Most Sprocker's are very easy to train, given their genuine willingness to please and the fact that they are greedy.

Now back to the inquisitive Sprocker. First you and other household members need to decide boundaries for your dog. These are the parts of the house and garden they are allowed to roam free in.

Upstairs or downstairs?

Are you going to let your dog upstairs in your home? A lot of people consider this out of bounds. There is no reason why your dog should be in the main bedroom part of the house. A nice clean soft bed is a great incentive for a naughty dog to jump and fall asleep on (rather like Goldilocks). If you choose to let them, then I personally don't have anything to argue with since my personal dog Bill, sleeps on my feet....and I like it....

BUT that's not everybody's idea of good behavior. I would like to point out that he is the only one of our dogs that does this (apart from Bob and Bubbles), and this is simply because I didn't know any better when I bought him and the second he started crying I dragged him off the floor and onto the bed....I would not do it now but hey ho...

So if upstairs is out of bounds then you will need to put a barrier across the stairs as a visual NO to your Sprocker. Do not use child gates, their rungs are too far apart and the perfect size for a pup to stick their head in and get stuck, and then howl like a banshee, frightening the life out of you and getting various family members in hysterics. Yes this has happened to us too. A puppy gate is perfect but you must drill the house team not to leave it open.

When you have decided which rooms are dog rooms, you need to do an 'accident waiting to happen' inventory on your hands and knees. There are plenty of places a puppy can get wedged, down the side of a cooker, a fridge, a cupboard, they can chew through electric cables in a trice, they can get their collars caught up on hooks or door knobs (we take any collars off whilst in the house), they can get curtain ties and blind pulls wrapped round their necks (and can strangle themselves very quickly). A lot of dogs are great at opening cupboard doors with their paws so child locks can be useful.

If you live near a busy road, it's best not to let the dog roam near your main door. All dogs are easily distracted and the last thing you want is to come home after a hard day, open your front door and have your dog charge out.

Laundry rooms can sometimes be an ok dog bed area however again the electric wires MUST be nowhere near the ground. Also washing machines and tumble driers can be

'Coco' owned by the Hollis family

very noisy and frightening to a young dog, and you also have the possibility of the puppy crawling into an open machine....

Personally we would recommend a kitchen. They are usually the soul of a home, got the right flooring and close to water and dog food etc. Put a puppy gate up on the doorway so you can leave the door open when you are not in there, and the pup can watch what's going on in the rest of the house.

It's a hands and knees job in here too. Move all cables, and close up escape routes to behind fridges etc. You can use a puppy pen to make a safe space for the pup to be whilst you are not in there, or too busy to watch him.

Crate training:

This has come very popular with puppy buyers. I can't remember it being around when we first had dogs, and I have to say I was not too keen on it in the beginning. We do 'crate' train pups for  people here, the theory being that its best they get used to going in and out of a crate from the earliest time in their lives possible so it becomes second nature.

Having done this the last few years I have come around to the benefits of it. I still can't quite get over the shallowness of the fact that I think they are really ugly but they are useful. It's a good place for a pup and a dog to call their own, a sanctuary for them to retreat to if need be. A safe place to lock them away for a short while, if you suddenly have to rush out.

I use my daughters to help with the crate training, I stick them and the very young puppies inside together (I do leave the door open) and let the pups have a fuss from them. After this we put an open crate in the kennels with their bed and blankets in and the pups take themselves in and out.

So if you are going to use a crate, then it needs to reside in your puppy's 'area' or 'safe place'. We suggest putting your pups bed inside it, along with some blankets that smell of his siblings and Mother, around this (outside of the crate) some newspaper for 'accidents' and then a water bowl and subsequent food bowl.

If you have had a puppy / dog before then you don't need to read this bit: Puppies and young dogs can take a shine to things they are not supposed to.

However there is no point telling them off after the fact since it is completely meaningless to them. They need to be caught mid-misdemeanor and verbally told off in the deepest gruffest voice you can muster. High pitched squealing at them doesn't cut it. They also do not like being made to maintain eye contact with you, so it's a combination of deep cross voice and eye contact.

For the record these are the things to keep out of the way of a nosy Sprocker:

- Loo rolls – such fun!
- Papers, books, magazines, homework etc. – these shred delightfully well.
- Play-doh and Lego – one chewy and one crunchy.
- Tablecloths dangling their edges off the sides of the kitchen/dining table – we don't need to explain this one.

- Children gesticulating holding pieces of food – this equals sore fingers and crying child.
- Long hair – any long hair should be tied back when playing with a puppy.

This phase doesn't always happen, some puppies are practically perfect in every way. Some, however, are a little naughty until they grow up.

The great outdoors:

Sprocker's are great diggers. It can be a bit of a hobby, but it is one you really need to clamp down on especially if you are garden proud. Sprocker's are also excellent hurdlers, only over upright fences, but they can reach

Maud' owned by Julian Hammond. The irrefutable proof that Sprockers can fly…..

surprising height even given the fact they might have short hairy legs.

So you might need to reconsider your fences. Going over and going under. Mainly make sure there are no holes at the bottom of the fence that look very inviting. If you feel that  your boundary fencing might be too low, this can be remedied by ending an extra line of tape, bunting, colored string etc. at a jaunty angle (see photo). This has been tried and tested here so we are sticking with it as our best form of defense. If it stops Ernie (Wise) the Chocolate Sprocker – it should deter most.

If you have any fruit trees in your garden, just be aware that Sprocker's are good fruit pickers, there is nothing quite as fun as throwing yourself at any long hanging branches, grabbing them and giving them a thorough shake. And (of course) eating whatever falls off. …this can lead to runny tummies.

There are quite a few poisonous plants – the Dogs Trust website has a great list so take a look on there.

www.dogstrust.org.uk

If you would like to avoid using your lawn as an outdoor loo then there are ways round this. Decide where the pups 'outside loo' will be. Preferably somewhere that is already concreted or flag stoned.

Ideally you would make this into an outdoor puppy pen, (you can also cover the inside area with shingle that can be easily scooped up along with the poo) which you put your puppy in after eating and just wait for him to do his 'business'.

The best way to begin with is to put him on a lead, and walk him into the area. This is not playtime so try and keep everything as low key as possible. The split second he starts to wee etc. then praise him calmly. As long as you take him to the same place after every meal he will learn that this is the place for his toilet, not the garden or house.

Essential Kit:

Now it's time to go shopping! Here are the basics:

Collar – don't go over the top with the pup's first collar. They are very good at taking them off and then chewing them. If you do have the inclination to go and order a bespoke handcrafted leather collar

then it is best to wait until the pup is full grown. You have been warned. All dogs must have an identity tag on their collars by law now. I would recommend not putting the dog's name on it, just yours and as many contact numbers as you can fit on. You don't want any potential dog thieves knowing your dog's name, do you?

Lead – we use a very light weight lead attached to the collar for training purposes. We attach it, and let the pup potter about with it on with us watching VERY carefully from the side lines.

However for walking purposes we use a light weight puppy sized slip lead, which does not attach to the collar, just over the pups head.

Crate – these are very useful for car journeys. Its stops the need for dog guards, which in our experience only serve as a Mensa test for any self-respecting dog. There is nothing that delights a dog

more than wiggling through the dog guard from the boot of the car to the back seat like a canine Houdini.

There are various different sizes of crates. Please make sure it fits in your boot of your car before you purchase it…the crate for the house (much easier to have two otherwise going out in the car will become more complicated) can be as big as you like. You will need a mat for both of them, plain flat ones that can just be chucked in a washing machine.

Water and food bowls – non slip are the best otherwise your pup will delight in clanging it around the kitchen like they are in an Olympic Curling competition. Heavier the better too. This stops the need for pup to pick them up and empty them for you. Food bowls don't matter so much but you will become very annoyed by water bowls being picked up and emptied on your feet. Stainless steel might not be the prettiest you can find but it is the hardiest, can be washed up with boiling water and/or put in a dishwasher. You can buy those specially shaped bowls specifically for spaniels which are cone shaped and designed so floppy ears don't fall into the food.

Bed – start small puppy size first so it's cozy. Make sure it is easily machine washed. So material yes, wicker no…pups love shredding wicker baskets.

Toys – in our experience you don't need too many of these. Ernie and Flo's favorites have been Kong toys, balls on rope, cotton rag toys and things to chew.

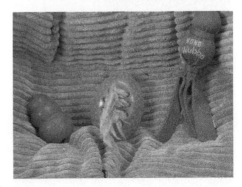

Avoid squeaky toys. They will drive you mad and not particularly safe if the pup manages to remove the squeaky thing from the middle and swallows it.

Food – make sure you have got what the breeder is feeding the puppy on: either buy some from them or make sure it is stocked locally. We go from a puppy to junior feed before they leave, and then we suggest keeping them on the junior food for six months and then weaning onto adult food of the owners choice.

Grooming kit –
Sprocker's are very good at self –cleaning (sometimes this can involve furniture). They don't need expensive trips to the grooming parlour, just a weekly

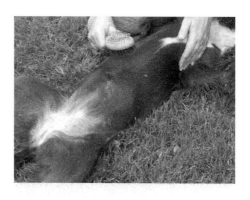

brush with a soft brush, and a comb. We do recommend getting a flea comb too...'just in case'. It is also advisable to use a puppy shampoo since these are all designed with sensitive canine skin in mind.

Other bits of kit....

Poo bags – these are very essential for when you start walking your puppy in public places. You can also buy pouches that attach to the lead, in which you can carry your poo bags. We sometimes use nappy bags if we run out but these are not as strong and much more likely to break.

Nail clippers – dogs that get walked on hard surfaces tend to wear their nails down themselves unlike their country cousins that will need a pedicure every now and then. Do ask your vet to show you first before you attempt it. There are blood vessels down into the dogs nails and if you cut too much off the nail will bleed, your dog will yelp and you will feel awful.

Treat bags – if you are planning on using treats as a training aid then just shoving them in your pocket is not a good idea (I know from lots of experience). You can buy especially made bags from pets stores or you improvise.

Dog food bins – these are made to take a big bag of dog food, have clip down air tight lids and a scoop. So far none of our dogs have managed to break into one so they are quite reliable!

That's it – you should be ready to go!

8 LIVING WITH YOUR PUPPY

Bringing puppy home:

You need a small bag of emergency equipment for the drive home. We normally don't feed our pups in the morning they are leaving (morning is the best time) to eliminate the chances of vomit.

But bring a couple of towels, plastic carrier bags and some wet wipes to mop up any spillage.

Morning is best so you can have a whole day settling your new puppy in. It is also best for there only to be two of you in the car, I appreciate that homecoming is a big thing but you don't want to overwhelm him with too much excitement and noise in one go. The passenger should put a towel on their lap, puppy on the towel, holding on firmly. I would recommend putting a collar and a lead on the pup and having the lead wrapped round your hand. This is so your slippery puppy doesn't decide to take a nose dive towards the driver or an opening door.

Once you reach home, offer him some water and then take him to his outdoor loo, and calmly wait until he has a wee or suchlike. Lots of praise, then indoors to his new abode.

Now is the time to
introduce him to his
bed/crate with the nice
smelling blanket from him
mum and siblings. Put him
in and walk away.
Hopefully the excitement of
the day so far combined

with the smell of home will let him have a nap.

The rest of the day should be spent relatively quietly but
still keeping him up and about (you want him as tired as
possible for his first night away from his siblings). Show
him round his new home, but only the parts he is allowed
in and get started with your house training. Put him to bed
as late as possible having taken him outside for a final
toilet. Then shut the door, walk away and put a pillow over
your head. Some pups can shriek like the world is ending
all night, some pups just go to sleep as if nothing has
changed.

The first few days – begin to house train

Routine, routine and some more routine. This is all about
basic house training and general good manners. What
work you put in now makes a huge difference; the adage
'start as you mean to go on' was invented for puppies.

Training to newspaper: once mum has left our pups for the
majority of the time, we start the process of training to
newspaper. If you choose to do so, start collecting old

papers early. We are lucky in the fact that all my Mothers friends plus other kind hearted souls hoard their used papers for us and they appear over the main gate in bundles on a regular

basis. This usually leaves me catching up on world news on my hands and knees in the puppy kennel.

There is also the option of puppy pads you can buy at big pet stores. I would like to add that the record for shedding those to pieces is held by Jades Cocker pups in 2013. It took about 30 seconds to shred and much longer for me to clear up. We are sticking to paper.

The idea is that you cover your floor area that the puppy will inhabit with thick layers of newspaper (this is why kitchens and other non-carpeted rooms are best). Every time the pup wakes up or has been fed, put the pup on the paper and try and keep him there until he has relieved himself, lots of praise must be forthcoming. You then pick dirty paper up and then replace with clean.

As soon as the puppy gets used to the idea of the paper, he will run to it to relieve himself, again more praise. Very slowly you start to reduce the amount of paper, moving the paper area towards the door. In the long run, and with Mother Nature being nice, you would aim to have the kitchen/outside door open with some newspaper on the threshold and just outside the door too.

If you start toilet training outside too, this should all fall into place neatly. Just keep an eye on him after eating, hopefully he will start to gravitate towards the paper, at which point you whisk him outside.

You do need to stay with him though. A Sprocker will be mightily miffed if you take him outside and just leave him there. He is expecting to be kept company and to find the back door shut in his face, will just result in basic whining, no going to the toilet, and then coming in and relieving himself indoors.

The first few days - Feeding

Now food manners: always keep his water bowl clean and full so he can drink whenever he wants and he always knows where it is. I would advise putting it in a corner in the kitchen, otherwise family members are inclined to kick it over and swear at you for leaving said article in a stupid place. Sprockers do also have a habit of emptying water bowls so they can carry them round…..

Uggeshall Luna Eclipse…. the Empress of emptying water bowls…owned by the Raymond family.

His first meal at home is important. Before you put the dish down, let him sniff the dish and then lick a bit from your fingers (you might need to wet the food down a little if you are on pure biscuits). He needs to see you as the Fairy Godmother of the food bowl (or Godfather etc.) and that you are in charge.

Attempt to get him to sit: if you move your hand over his eyeline, puppies do tend to sit down. Then place the food in front of him. If he doesn't finish it (which is quite unlikely) then just take the remainder away.

It is now you need to keep him either on his newspaper if you are paper training, or outside if you are going straight to the outdoor method. Keep him moving about a little, but focused on toilet not play. When he finally goes, lots of quiet praise WHILST he is doing it. Ecstatic praise is saved for the really clever stuff like 'sit' or 'stay'.

At this young age he will still be on three meals a day. So you will find your life revolving around feeding, playing and getting on with the house training. Your perseverance will pay off so don't get disheartened.

The first few days – walking and grooming

The best thing is to get pup used to be being bathed and brushed from an early age. When they are really little we use the kitchen sink, but once they get to squirming size then the bath with a non-slip mat is the best bet. Always use a puppy shampoo, otherwise you might find your pups skin gets very irritated.

They do not need a lot of brushing at this point, but it's good to get them used to the idea of it. So use a soft brush all over his body once a day will get him used to being fully handled and will stand you in good stead for later in life.

Walking

A good rule of thumb is for your puppy to have five minutes per day per month of age: so a three month old puppy would have five minutes x 3 equaling 15 minutes walking. You can do this twice a day. Pups do

get bored of being in the same place, that's usually when they might consider tunneling out and seeking adventure elsewhere so do think 'variety is the spice of life' for your young sprocker.

You can use this walk time as part of their socialization process. The more your pup sees at a young age the better. He needs to be introduced to absolutely everything you can muster. Start on quiet roads, and work up to busy noisy ones. Chat to policemen (missed this one out with Bubbles so she now woofs rather aggressively at any poor policemen. We have had a rather embarrassing moment when she got a young officer cornered in my Mothers bedroom....), firemen, postmen, people on bikes, horses that are being ridden, motor bikes and anything else you can think or and/or find.

Your first attempts at walking on a lead are going to be haphazard. So deep breath and don't expect to get very far. The main point is to be consistent. Some puppies fly off at 100 miles an hour, some puppies just spread eagle themselves on the ground and refuse to move.

Lots of reassurance is needed from you. Some treats in your pocket (Ernie spends his entire life gazing at my right hand pocket). Try to walk the pup between you and a fence, a wall or a line of trees so you have a narrow corridor for the pup to keep to. Keep the lead short and upright and gently persuade the puppy that walking beside you is the safest option.

Your goal is not to let the puppy pull. So basically every time the pup pulls away from you, you stop. When you stop the pup will usually turn to see why he can't move forwards anymore, making the lead slacken. At this moment you immediately praise him and then continue walking for as long as the lead stays loose.

The process is then repeated. And probably repeated a few times more. However your patience will be rewarded in the long run, the more effort you put in now, the easier everything else will fall into place.

Letting puppy off the lead:

This always worries a few of our new puppy owners, the idea of letting the puppy off the lead, and then he disappears off into the distance never to be seen again. As far as I know it is has never happened.

You need to think of yourself as the pups replacement pack. After spending some time with you, the puppy will consider you as their 'safe house' and not run off from you.

'Coco' owned by Lucy Hollis and family.....here she is contemplating the great outdoors.

In the meantime (in between vaccinations for example) you can work on your recall about the home). Start in the same room as the pup, treats in your pocket, call his name and show him the treat and he will coming running to you (you can start using your whistle here too – more information on whistle training later on).

When he arrives in front of you, lots of praise and a treat and so you carry on. You can work up to being in other rooms, top of the garden wherever it is feasible for you pup to find you from. As he gets better, less use of the treats just keep up the praise.

If you are still worried about letting him off in the big outdoors, then retractable leads are your way forwards for a little while. It won't take long for trust to be built up and then you can go for a 'proper' Sprocker walk which entails them running ahead and then circling back just to check you are too not far away!

Recall:

When we are training our pups we always use a whistle as well as verbal commands. This is so our pups and dogs come back to a pure whistle but also their name, which is vital since I often go out without my whistle.

However whistle training is great for various reasons:

First it saves your voice, it travels much further than your dulcet bellowing can, and it's short, sharp and effective and will hide any trace of negative emotion in your voice.

You can also train to sit and stay at a distance, which always looks good. It means that the dog will always respond to the whistle, so it doesn't matter who walks him if he is pre-programmed to come back to that particular pitch

NB whistles come in different pitches. It is advisable to just buy a couple of the same one to begin with (it does not matter which pitch) and keep one as a spare. It you are going to be really clever and later on you have more than one dog, you can have a different pitch for a different dog. Then you have to remember to put both whistles round your neck.....and which whistle is which.....

The main thing to remember is to have your whistle around

your neck (I do appreciate this sounds obvious but if you are not used to it, it is easily forgotten). As an aside I would like to also mention that our goats, sheep and ponies are also trained to come charging to a whistle. It was not planned like that but it is surprisingly efficient!

So you call the puppy by his name, and then a short sharp two blasts on the whistle. Carry on doing this for a few weeks, and then try just blowing the whistle. If he returns just to the whistle, job done. If he doesn't then you just need a bit more time practicing.

When you have both mastered this, you can go and hide around the house and then blow the whistle. Depending on your hiding skills you might need to call a few times…but he will find you (and be very pleased with himself).

In the meantime you can also work on the 'Sit' command. There are two options here:

First have a titbit in your
hand, with the pup as near
to you are possible. Show
him the titbit up high, he
should naturally sit to look
up to you. As he does this,
say the word 'Sit' as his
bottom hits the ground.

Lots of praise and the treat ensue.

Second way is minus the treat. Have the dog standing as

close to you as possible, if you hold your palm out over his line of vision he should naturally sit to be able to look up to you, and regain eye contact. Same as before, as his bottom hits the ground say the word 'Sit' and lots of praise.

You can now start bringing in the whistle too if you plan on using it. As you say the word 'Sit' follow immediately with one short sharp burst of the whistle. I find it easier to have the whistle in my mouth between my teeth whilst I do this.

Car travel:

Car travel should start as soon as possible. Your pup will have had his first experience on his journey home which hopefully was a good experience for him. Young dogs can often suffer from motion sickness but it is likely that this is caused more by nervousness of the situation than the actual car itself.

So the more you take him out the better. When he is really little it is better to keep him on your lap. Lead and collar on, with a towel between you and him 'just in case'. Later, when the puppy is more confident, it is important that the puppy/dog is restrained in some way for everyone's safety. We would recommend a cage in the back, as opposed to dog guards. If you have a cage that fits snugly in the back of the car and inside this have some bedding, then this is the safest way. If you were to brake suddenly you would want the cage and puppy to have minimal movement.

You can also buy dog seatbelts, which do work for some

dogs. Some sit serenely in the car with the belt on, some get very excited and try and twist round in it. All of our dogs go in cages, and if we leave the car open at any point we will often find it full of dogs looking expectantly at us. My Mothers dog particularly likes waiting for her in front of the steering wheel. It clearly makes him feel important.

It is important to take your pup and dog out and about, only short journeys when they are little and great expeditions when they are older. Even if it's just the school run, or a quick shopping trip, they do love to be involved and it's incredibly good for them in many ways.

Do remember to leave the windows open a little when you are driving, just for a bit of air. Never leave the window open enough for them to be able to bail out. It has not happened to us, but it has to an acquaintance. It is never good to leave a dog in the car even on a warm day, even with windows open; a car makes a good dog oven.

Preventative and general health care:

These are basically things to do on a regular basis to help keep your puppy/dog healthy and avoid any unnecessary trips to the vet.

Ears – Sprocker's have beautiful ears, but they are one of the common problem factors in many Spaniels. Checking they are clean and/or cleaning them weekly makes a big difference. First thing to do is have a quick smell. If they smell foul then it's a trip to the vets: they might have an infection and bacteria in their ears.

It is good to get your
Sprocker used to having
their ears cleaned once a
week if you can. Never
use cotton buds or
cotton wool. You need
to use the flat cotton
pads that 'one' would use
for make up or taking off nail varnish.

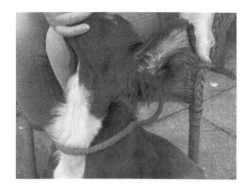

You should be able to get a good ear cleaning solution
from your local pet store. For the first few times, start by
just giving your puppy a head massage, incorporating his
ears, so he gets used to the idea of you feeling all around
and in his ears.

When you think he is
ready gently pull the ear
flap upward to straighten
out the ear canal, and
then squirt some of the
solution into your
puppy's ear. Massage the
base with your fingers
for about 30 seconds (you should be able to hear it
squelching), making sure the cleaning solution gets deep
down into the ear.

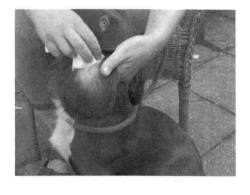

At this point your puppy is going to be desperate to have a
good shake of the head to get rid of that solution out of his
ear. Keeping hold of him (i.e. collar and lead job, you don't

want him running off), let him have a little shake before you start cleaning with the cotton pad (you might want to pull yourself back a bit at this point, canine ear solutions don't taste very nice and sting your eyes).

Use a damp cotton pad to gently wipe out the dogs ears and clean them as best you can. Make sure you don't poke anything down into the ear itself. All you need to do now is make sure they air dry! So preferably out and about in the fresh air.

If you don't feel confident doing this yourself the first time, then it is worth asking your vet to show you how to do it.

If you notice your Sprocker doing a lot of vigorous scratching of the ears, it probably means he has ear mites. This is another vet visit. However a lot of the new worming tablets now encompass worms, fleas and ear-mites so it would be worth paying a bit extra for the future when you next have to worm your dog.

Do keep your Sprocker ears brushed on a regular basis, the hair in this area can so easily get knotted and tangled and pull on itself, causing discomfort. You can trim with sharp scissors the hair on the inside of the ear flap. This is best done once you can trust your Sprocker to stand still. Sometimes a second person to hold onto him whilst you do something like this will make the whole process a lot easier.

Eyes - eyes are so delicate on any of us so if you are ever unsure what is going on with your Sprockers eyes, then it is a vet visit. The one ailment you can deal with is

Conjunctivitis; this is the term for inflammation, discomfort and reddening of the eye often most noticeable by the eye weeping, or being partially closed up by a thin film crust. You can use boiling water with salt, wait for it to cool down to body temperature and using a cotton pad gently soak the eye, removing slowly the puss or crust.

Worms

Roundworms: all puppies should be wormed fortnightly from two weeks to three months of age, then monthly up to six months of age. After that your pet Sprocker should be wormed twice a year.

Tapeworms: These need a guest pass (hosts) which is usually given by your dog's fleas (if they have any). Hence using a multi worming tablet (we use Stronghold) which keeps different types of worms at bay, as well as fleas and ear-mites. It might be a little more costly but it is certainly worth every penny.

Fleas

As long as your breeder handed you over a flea free puppy, this is all about prevention rather than cure. If you use the multipurpose worming tablet, which also combats fleas, you should not ever have a problem. You do need to keep any eye on other dogs if they are visiting your home; fleas are very good at jumping from one dog to another!

If you did invest in a flea comb, then it's certainly worthwhile having a 'flea-check' when you groom your

Sprocker. Fleas like to hide down by the dog's tail, around the collar area and if you turn your dog belly side up, you might be able to see a few scampering away from the lower belly / genital area where the coat is finer.

We use a flea comb and a bucket of tepid water, gently but firmly pull the comb through the coat (we start on the belly up side) and then dunk any fleas or grit in the water and then comb again. If there are fleas, they will scurry off into the thicker part of the coat, so you turn the dog over and comb through there etc.

In the warmer months all our dogs go swimming in the river in the field, this is a great way to give the dogs a simple clean and to help fleas float away. Washing with shampoo is something that needs to be done only now and then, you don't wish to clean the coat of too many of its essential goodness.

Vaccinations

Vaccines are basically a modified live, or killed, form of the infection which does not cause illness in the dog, but instead stimulates the formation of antibodies against the disease itself.

The five major diseases are:

- Canine distemper
- Infectious canine hepatitis
- Leptospirosis
- Canine parvovirus

- Kennel cough

Many vaccination courses now include a component against parainfluenza virus, one of the causes of kennel cough, which is not a good thing for your dog to have at all! A separate vaccine against bordetella, another cause of kennel cough can be given in droplet form down the nose by your vet. Your dog will spend the rest of the day glaring at you, but it's worth a sulky Sprocker so you can rest assured that you are vaccinated up to the hilt.

Puppy should have their first vaccination at 8 weeks approximately and a follow up dose 2 to 4 weeks later. It is at this point you can have the separate kennel cough vaccine. After that you need to have your Sprocker booster jabs on a yearly basis. Most good breeders will not let their puppy's leave until they have been vet checked and had their first lot of eight week vaccines.

Feeding and dog treats

A good food for your dog will bring health and happiness all round. There is no point in feeding your beloved Sprocker a poor quality food. However some of the medium priced brands that you can buy in the Supermarkets can do just as well as some of the high price bracket ones you might see sold at your vets.

With any luck your puppy will not require any specialized food types however quite a few dogs can be wheat and gluten intolerant and this can differ from one pup only in an entire litter. This also might be something that doesn't become apparent until the puppy starts growing up.

We use a very high quality, sensitive puppy and junior food for the first six months. It is wheat and gluten free and packed full of everything your puppy needs to grow in every sense. We find it is usually when the puppy/young dog moves from a junior food to an adult food that such intolerances can become apparent.

Changing from one brand to another needs to be done slowly otherwise you will end up with runny stools and an upset stomach.

Do not worry about feeding the same food to your puppy all the time; puppies are not like us humans when it comes to food stuffs so they won't get bored!

The amount you feed your puppy each feed time is an individual calculation based on the puppies weight and should be based on the manufactures guidelines which will be on the bag itself.

They need to be on three meals a day up to about nine months and then down to two. Some people will then cut this down at about eighteen months to one meal a day but that is a personal choice for you. Our dogs get two meals a day; we just split the amount they should be having per day into two.

There are two main popular types of food you can give your puppy now. Firstly is the dry complete dog biscuit which has everything in it your pup and dog will need. Secondly (and gaining momentum in interest) is the raw food diet. This is simply raw meat, bones , fruit , vegetables, raw eggs and sometimes dairy all ground up and frozen in containers. They have been quite controversial, but the popularity is rising. The idea is that dogs will thrive on an evolutionary diet based on what canines ate before they were domesticated.

Potential risks which have been mentioned is a threat to human and dog health from bacteria in raw meat, and that this unbalanced diet (in their eyes) may damage the health of the dog.

What is boils down to for you, is that use whichever feels most sensible and right for you.

Treats

There are lots of treats on the market, from the supermarket to the vets practice. It does seem to be that some people feel you shouldn't need to use a treat to train a dog, or to reward him for good behavior.

I like giving the dogs a treat. For good behavior, doing what they are told and just simply because it makes me feel good too! I make our own dog treats and then freeze them.

However that doesn't mean I don't buy a supermarket packet every now and then too.

9 IN PRAISE OF SPANIELS

Cocker Love – *by Vera Page*

There's a love that lingers always

Deep within my heart

Its the love for cocker spaniels,

Here's how it got to start.

Bought a puppy, silky coated,

Eyes of brown that looked to me

Like he thought I was an idol

Showed his trust and faith in me.

Stubby tail that wagged 'hello there!'

Every time he heard my step

Fitted his mood right in with my moods-

Quiet, or a lot of pep.

Ears that gratefully extended

Quite a ways towards the ground

Chasing after balls: retrieving

Anything he found around

Gentle always with children

As he grew from puppy hood

Into just the kind of dog folks

Liked throughout the neighbourhood.

I'm a hunter and I love it,

So did that first cocker pup-

Didn't really have to time to train him,

He just seemed to pick it up.

Years have passed, but still that puppy

In my heart has left a trace,

For every time I lose a cocker

Another one must take its place

Recipe for Springer Spaniels

C 2006 - by Shelby Gomez (as told to Lillian Seldeen)

Once upon a time
... In Mother Nature's kitchen,
She was whipping up some batches,
Of puppies and little kittens.

She gathered all her recipes,
Ingredients and such,
And set about creating
With her very special touch.

Each recipe was different,
So she meted out with care,
Double checking all her measurements,
To be sure she did not err.

Labradors and Shepherds,
Pomeranians, Maltese;
Alley cats and Maine Coon Cats,
Persian and Siamese.

She worked all day and
Into night;
She cooked them to perfection.
She smiled with pride, took great delight,
In each delicate confection.

Soon the sun was rising,
Her kitchen was a mess;
Still she had to make the Springers;
Before she'd finally rest.

But as she started stirring,
She felt a little hazy;
And instead of just a dash,
She added half a cup of crazy!

She realized her mistake too late,
There was no going back;
She'd have to figure out a way
To get things back on track.

She grabbed "The Joy of Cooking",
And started flipping through;
And there she found the answer,
Of what she had to do.

To balance out the crazy,
She added lots of smarts;
And being on the safe side;
She gave them all big hearts.

Warm eyes, smooth coats,
And goofy smiles galore;
She folded in a singing voice,
For all folks to adore.

A wiggle butt that never stops,
A tail that always wags;
"Only the best ingredients";
She simply had to brag.

And from the highest cupboard,
A little this and that;
Agility, obedience,
The ability to track.

Exhausted but contented,
She popped them in the oven;
Then pulled out Springer Spaniels,
Full of sugar, spice and lovin'.

Now her job was almost done,
Just one thing for good measure;
She labeled each and every one,
"Mother Nature's Little Treasure".

Willow

Willow the chocolate Sprocker (AKA the Chocolate Rocket) came to live with us in December 2013. She has developed some annoying habits but mostly endearing ones. She puts herself to bed each  night with no fuss but unfortunately in lue of this good behavior will proceed to patiently pull the stuffing out of the corner of her bed piece by piece.

She loves the beach and any form of water. Her last big splash was in the canal through Tivorton, Devin where she submerged herself like an otter and reappearing with the ease of a mermaid.

She loves everybody, and everybody who meets her loves her.

By Kathy Raison

Archie

With his stunning good looks and friendly mischevious nature, Archie is a true 'showman' and entertains wherever he goes. He was the naughtiest puppy ever

to grace the doors of the obedience club but he has turned out to be the most well rounded friend and companion I could have wished for who, astonishingly has obtained his Kennel Club 'gold test' for obedience.

He particularly loves smoked salmon and parma ham wrapped around asparagus, no one has quite got through to him that this strictly NOT Archie food, however he is so quick and innocent, stolen in a blinding flash, that it is hard to believe he stole from under ones watchful gaze.

Archie is bright and strong and my constant companion, in the shooting season he 'picks up' several times a week and during the summer he swims in the sea. But the most important thing about Archie is how much I love him and he, in turn, loves me.

By Amanda Pratt – owner of Archie

Chester

The world according to Chester by Anne-Marie

Chester was the smallest of the litter by quite a margin which, at some points in his life with us, deemed him used in various ways by his siblings. Soft pillow, battering ram, step and anything else they could imagine. But it never fazed him. He would always wiggle through the mob, sneaking headfirst into the feed bowl. Never missed a 'Good Morning' sighting of me, charging out of the throng tail held as high as possible, continuously cheerful smiling up at me even on a really grotty day. Certainly the shyest pup, he took a while to trust visitors but look at him now....I am very proud of him.

My Chester by Lynn Chaplin

When I first met Chester he was curled up hiding between his brothers. He was so small compared to them, but you certainly wouldn't think of this now looking at his picture. He has filled out and grown into a fine handsome dog, still the most affectionate Sprocker with whom we love to cuddle and he loves to cuddle us.

Johnny

And last but certainly never the least here is 'Johnny' who is owned by Mike and Sue Parkinson. Anyone who ever meets this irrepressible Sprocker will never forget him, he was the leading actor in his litter and his notorious  full-on happy character gets bigger and brighter by the day.

10 A GALLERY OF SPROCKERS

'Willow' – owned by Kathy and Terry Raison

'Maud' (AKA the Sprocker that flies) owned by Julian Hammond and family

'Chester' owned by Lynn Chaplin

'Murphy' owned by Lindsey Hallgarth

'Murphy' owned by Angela Last

'Archie' owned by Amanda Pratt

'Bramble' owned by Darcy Murray

'Monty' owned by Anna Gardiner

'Charlie and Millie' owned by Donnie Shaw

'Jasper' owned by Alexandra Ackroyd

'Maggie' owned by Lucy Gilkes

'Oscar' owned by Maria Goodby

'Rhubarb' owned by Juliet Hughes

Elly and 'Tai' – Tai owned by Shereen Osbourne

'Breeze' owned by the Stammers family

'Toffee' owned by the Atherton family

'Mabel' owned by the English family

'Fletcher' owned by the Ryder family

'Rosie and Dixie' owned by Jackie and Nigel Millins-Horne

'Pebbles' owned by the Robinsons.

'Johnny' owned by Mike and Sue Parkinson

ABOUT THE AUTHORS

Anne-Marie Millard and Richard Botwright own and run 'Uggeshall Kennels' in North Suffolk. From here they breed working Springer's, Cockers and Sprockers as well as train young part trained dogs.

Anne-Marie is an established author with seven already internationally selling non-fiction books translated into 12 differing languages.

Richard is an ex gamekeeper with decades of experience in the shooting and dog training world.

They live at their small-holding with Anne-Maries children and Mother, creating a three generation household under one roof. Combining this with various other animals wandering round, it is a great place to gain insight, information and to spend both their working lives and personal days with their shared passion of the Spaniel in all its shapes and forms.

Printed in Great Britain
by Amazon

40095690R00047